Earth and the Solar System

Contents

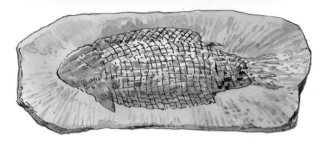

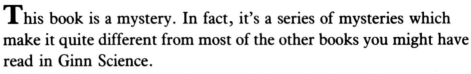

Introduction

This book is a mystery. In fact, it's a series of mysteries which make it quite different from most of the other books you might have read in Ginn Science.

Most of the science you have read about has been discovered and then checked and re-checked by scientists all over the world. As far as anyone can tell, most of it is fact and we are unlikely to find evidence which disproves many of the ideas, no matter how long we look.

This isn't true of all science though. There are plenty of areas where scientists don't know the whole truth; where an enormous amount of investigation and experimentation is still needed if we are to advance our knowledge much further.

The science of the Earth and space is one of those areas. Unlike many of the Ginn Science books, this one is filled with words such as 'might', 'probably' and 'could have'. The writer's choice of language reflects the uncertainty of our knowledge of the Earth's history and the universe of which planet Earth is just one very, very, very tiny part.

Some things we can say with a degree of certainty. There have been ice ages and other periods during which the shape of the Earth's surface has been formed and re-formed. We can tell from looking closely at fossils and where they were found, roughly how

Follow this line over the next few pages to find out what it tells you about the development of the planet on which you live . . .

4500 million years ago
Planet Earth was a ball of molten rock.

4300 — 4100 million years ago
Meteorites bombarded the Earth. Poisonous gases swirled around the surface. Lethal ultraviolet rays zapped in from the sun. The Earth was slowly cooling and its crust was hardening. Volcanoes poured out lava and ash. Water condensed in the atmosphere.

long ago the original animals or plants must have lived. We know that some rocks were formed in different ways to others. We know, too, of the existence of other planets within our solar system and we know that our solar system is just one part of a large galaxy, which is itself just one of a number of other large galaxies.

But there is much that we don't know. How many animals lived on the Earth millions of years ago for which there are no fossil remains? What were they like? What effect did they have upon each other and upon the development of our planet? How accurate is the picture we draw of the Earth then?

Space, too, contains its own questions. How did the universe, of which planet Earth is a part, even begin? Why does every object have its own gravity? How big is the galaxy which contains all of our solar system and more? How many more galaxies are there stretching millions and millions of kilometres into space? Can we even begin to imagine a space so big that we can't tell whether it has an end?

This Ginn Science book can't answer those questions. It can give you, though, an insight into some of the most thrilling and difficult questions scientists will ever try to answer. Those scientists are on a long, probably never-ending, journey of discovery. This book might help you join them.

4000 million years ago
The Earth was still cooling. Hot water collected in rivers and shallow seas. Lightning raged in the sky.

3700 million years ago
The first living things appeared in shallow seas. They were organisms with single cells, like bacteria, and perhaps viruses. They made oxygen as a waste product.

Planet Earth

Seen from space, our planet, the Earth, looks very beautiful. White clouds streak and swirl across the greens of vegetation, the blues of water and the browns of sand and rock. Islands, continents and oceans pattern its surface.

No humans had ever had the chance to gaze down at the Earth until the first astronauts orbited the planet in the 1960s. The view from the outside has changed our knowledge of the planet. We now have new ways of measuring and observing what is happening on the Earth's surface. Using satellites, scientists can watch the weather patterns as they form and follow the movement of the polar ice-caps. We can check the health of crops and forests and measure the spread of flood waters or pollution from an industrial site. The gases in the outer layers of our atmosphere can now be studied.

Being able to watch our planet from the outside has helped change the way we think about the Earth. It is easier to see that three-quarters of the planet is under water. Of the quarter that is land, we can see that a third of the land is desert and that a lot of the rest is ice, mountains or swamps.

It is also easier to understand that all things on our planet depend on each other. Air, water, soil and all living things are connected, like a great delicate web. The surface of this planet with its water, soil and air is where we all live. Here, in a very narrow band around the Earth, is everything on which we depend. In the past few years, we have realized more and more just how important this band is. We know now that every part of the planet is precious to the survival of life.

". . . looks like a beautiful jewel in space.
Neil Armstrong from Apollo 11, 1969

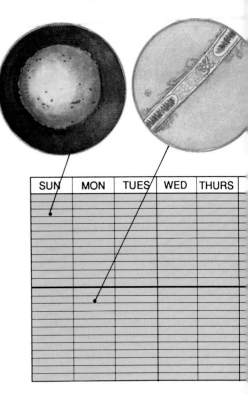

SUN	MON	TUES	WED	THURS

3500 million years ago
Single-celled organisms were flourishing underwater.

This map of the universe is 400 years old. It shows how people used to think of the Earth as the centre of the universe.

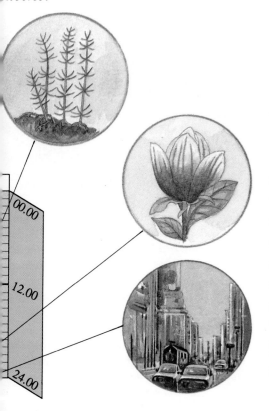

Not very long ago people believed that our planet was the very centre of the universe. They thought that the Earth stayed still while the sun, moon and stars moved around it. As we lie in bed or sit eating a meal, the floor beneath us does seem still. Understanding that we are whizzing and turning through space is really very difficult.

But we now know that the Earth is just one of nine known planets turning around a star and that this star is an average-sized star orbiting within a vast collection of stars called a galaxy. We have given some stars names. We call the star nearest to the Earth, 'the sun'. We know that our galaxy is one of about 100 000 million (100 000 000 000) other galaxies. We are not at the centre of the universe. We also know that the Earth is something like 4500 million (4 500 000 000) years old and that it is changing all the time.

These are exciting facts. Understanding them means thinking about vast numbers — huge distances in space, huge distances in time. It helps us to understand if we compare these huge numbers with something familiar and much smaller. Think, for example, of the seven days of a week: each day 24 hours long, each hour 60 minutes, each minute 60 seconds. If we compare the 4500 million years planet Earth has existed with one week, we can say that 7500 years of the Earth's history is equal to one second of the week.

Using the scale of a week, planet Earth began as a ball of molten rock in the early hours of the first day, Sunday. Living things appeared in warm pools of water around 3500 million (3 500 000 000) years ago or at half past one on Monday afternoon. But the first living things able to survive on dry land didn't appear until the last day of the week, around half past eight on Saturday morning. Flowers were here 100 million years (100 000 000) ago, at twenty past eight on Saturday evening. The last 2000 years of the Earth's history, the period which we know most about, take just over a quarter of a second, as midnight strikes on Saturday night.

3000 million years ago

The shaping of the Earth

The Earth is a ball of extremely hot metal, melted rock and heated rock with an outside shell of cold rock. At least, this is what scientists think. It is impossible for humans to dig down to the middle of the Earth. The temperature and pressure increase rapidly as you go down. The deepest mine is only a scratch on the Earth's surface. The inside of the Earth is probably arranged like a lightly boiled egg. The crust, the layer of rock on the surface, is thin like the shell of an egg. It is, on average, 32 kilometres thick. Beneath mountains it can be as much as 65 kilometres thick but under oceans it is much thinner, in places only five kilometres.

The layer of rock beneath the crust is called the mantle and is like the white of the egg. The centre of the Earth, called the core, is like the yolk. It is probably made of metal, iron mixed with nickel. The middle of the core is about 2500 kilometres across and could be solid metal under tremendous heat and pressure. The rest of the core, scientists think, is liquid. Scientists can find out about the unseen rocks beneath our feet by studying the shock waves from earthquakes and tracking the way they travel through the Earth.

The Earth probably began as a swirling mass of gas and dust which collected together into a ball and began heating up. Over millions of years, the surface cooled enough to form crusts, or scabs, of solid rock. Water vapour in the gases around the Earth condensed and fell as rain but boiled away in the great heat still being given out by the planet. After millions more years, the rock was cool enough for water to collect in hollows and dents which had formed on its surface.

The water began the slow and never-ending process of wearing the rocks away. At the same time, powerful forces inside the planet continued to make new rocks, forcing them up on to the surface. So the surface of the Earth — its appearance and the landscape — kept changing. It is still changing.

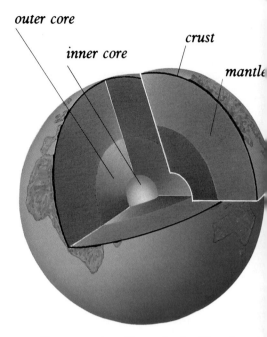

Cross-section through the Earth

outer core
inner core
crust
mantle

This island, called Surtsey, appeared quite suddenly off the coast of Iceland in 1963. It was formed from volcanic activity in the sea-bed. Within one month of it being formed, the molten rock had cooled enough for scientists to be able to land there and study the rocks. The lava was still steaming then but, after three years, the volcanic activity had died down. Now there are many species of plants and animals living on the 175 metre-high island.

2500 million years ago

2000 million years ago

lacier

Some changes are easy to see. Waves crash against cliffs, wearing them away. Pieces crack from the rock face where a road is cut through a hill, leaving scars of brighter-coloured, sharp-edged rock. A flooded river carries away earth and stones from the river bank.

Some of the changes made by big, dramatic events can also be seen, once you know what to look for. Four times in the last two million years, ice ages have gripped the world. At the height of the ice ages, ice sheets covered nearly a third of all land. **Glaciers** reached from the Arctic as far south as present-day London and New York and stretched up from the Antarctic as far north as Argentina and New Zealand. The glaciers ground the tops of mountains, gouged out wide, deep valleys and shoved huge quantities of soil and rock from one place to another.

Because so much of the world's water froze as ice, the level of the oceans dropped by about 180 metres. Grass grew where fish had swum. Stranded islands became joined up to the mainland. Shallow seas like the Baltic and the English Channel dried out. Britain became joined to the rest of Europe and Ireland joined on to Britain. The last ice age ended only about 10 000 years ago. The climate warmed so the ice melted and the seas rose. The seas drowned rivers and filled in valleys to form new bays and inlets. The water flooded over forests to remake the islands. Much of the way the United Kingdom, Northern Europe, Asia and North America look today was created by the events of the ice ages.

But the four great ice ages are only a wink of an eye in the Earth's history. During millions of years, land has risen above the sea, been thrust up into mountain ranges, been eroded back to low hills, then has sunk and been covered with water again. Other ice ages have held the Earth in extremely cold temperatures. Eroded rock, soil and decaying matter have settled on the bottom of lakes and around the edges of continents, creating new layers of rock. Volcanoes have spewed out hot ash and molten lava from supplies deep below the ground.

Earthquakes have shaken and cracked the rocks of the Earth's surface. The continents themselves have drifted across the surface of the Earth. They have been joined together, then separated. They are still moving, slowly. Australia is heading north and America is moving west gradually.

1800 million years ago

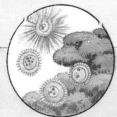

The Earth's history — hidden clues

When did life begin? What came first? When did creatures like us first appear? How long ago were the first dragonflies in the sky and mosses on the ground? Were they the same kinds of dragonflies and mosses as the ones we see today? Fossils are our only clue to the history of life before man's appearance on the Earth. We can only begin to piece the jigsaw together when the fossil remains of living things are found, miraculously preserved inside rocks or coal, tucked into mud, earth or sand, or thrown up by the tide on the seashore.

Fossils are scarce. Very few of the billions of plants and animals which have lived on the Earth ever became fossils. The conditions have to be just right to preserve flesh, shells, wings, bones, teeth, leaves, the pollen of a flower or the shape of a footprint.

Once fossils have formed, the rocks preserving them have to survive the endless, slow erosion processes and the movement of the Earth's surface. During tens of millions of years, the surface has been buckled, heaved and tilted, exploded in volcanoes and shaken by earthquakes. Land has sunk beneath the sea, then risen again, then sunk again. Mountains have been twisted up into raw ridges of rock, then gradually eroded back to flattened stumps. Glaciers have ground icy paths and carried material with them. Very few of the rocks containing fossils survive, least of all where we can find them.

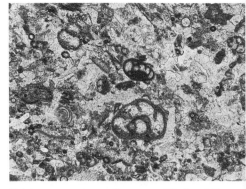

Limestone, greatly magnified with fossils of tiny sea creatures in it

This fossil fish is approximately 60 million years old. Its shape is very similar to that of the present-day perch in the picture above.

(Left) Fossilized seashells

1500 million years ago

1200 million years ago
The first living things with more than one cell appeared in shallow seas.

The fossil record is pure chance. Huge, frustrating gaps in our knowledge wait to be filled in. We only know about a tiny fraction of the creatures which have crawled on this Earth, swum in the waters or flown in the air. Dinosaurs are only some of the many living things which once roamed the planet then became extinct. Marvellous, unbelievable creatures can be discovered as fossils, every hair in place, each eye and claw, and quite unlike anything ever seen before.

Even tiny living things have been discovered as fossils. It is difficult to imagine finding fossilized bacteria but, in the 1950s, scientists realized that some rocks in Africa, Australia and America held the fossils of 3500 million year-old micro-organisms. They measured only one or two-hundredths of a millimetre across. Discovering the history of life on Earth is an exciting, developing science.

600 million years ago Creatures with shells appeared in the seas. There are many fossils of creatures and plants from this time on. 87% of the Earth's history to date had already passed.

The Fish

Like an angler on the river bank
With his back bent over his line
The colliery headgear with its steel rope
Fishes the ground for coal.

It fishes through millions of years
And half a mile of earth
With a cage to bring up its catch
From the forests of the past.

The silvery fossil of a lost species
On a lump of coal that was buried ages
Goes by on the conveyor too fast
To be saved from the crusher.

Stanley Cook

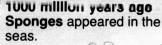
1000 million years ago
Sponges appeared in the seas.

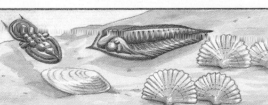

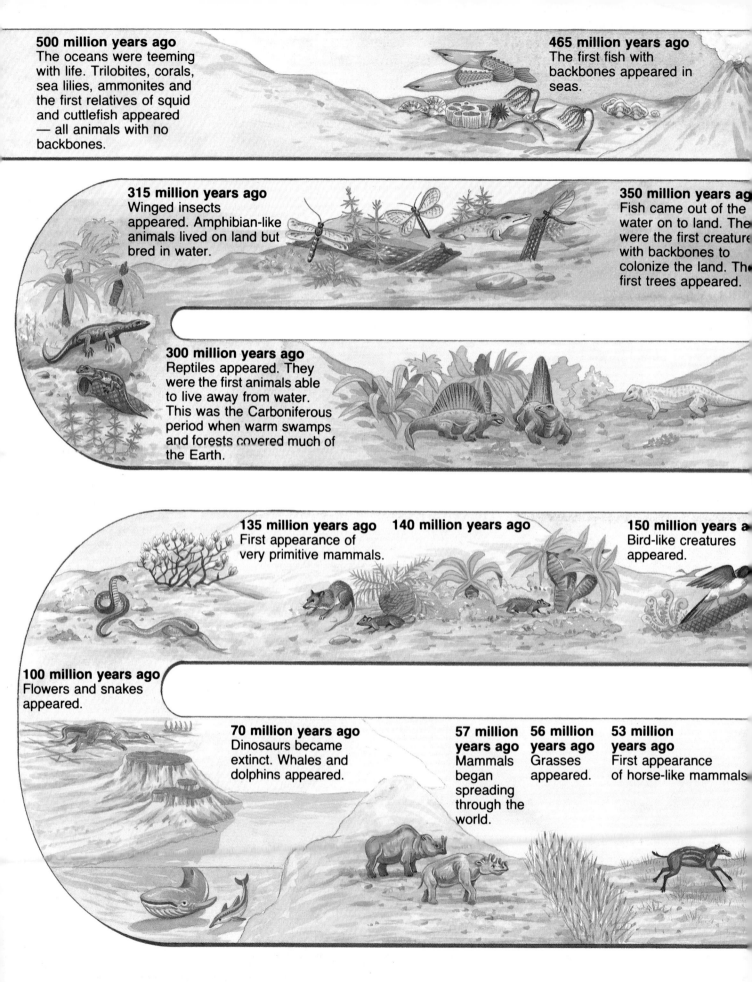

500 million years ago
The oceans were teeming with life. Trilobites, corals, sea lilies, ammonites and the first relatives of squid and cuttlefish appeared — all animals with no backbones.

465 million years ago
The first fish with backbones appeared in seas.

315 million years ago
Winged insects appeared. Amphibian-like animals lived on land but bred in water.

350 million years ago
Fish came out of the water on to land. They were the first creatures with backbones to colonize the land. The first trees appeared.

300 million years ago
Reptiles appeared. They were the first animals able to live away from water. This was the Carboniferous period when warm swamps and forests covered much of the Earth.

135 million years ago
First appearance of very primitive mammals.

140 million years ago

150 million years ago
Bird-like creatures appeared.

100 million years ago
Flowers and snakes appeared.

70 million years ago
Dinosaurs became extinct. Whales and dolphins appeared.

57 million years ago
Mammals began spreading through the world.

56 million years ago
Grasses appeared.

53 million years ago
First appearance of horse-like mammals.

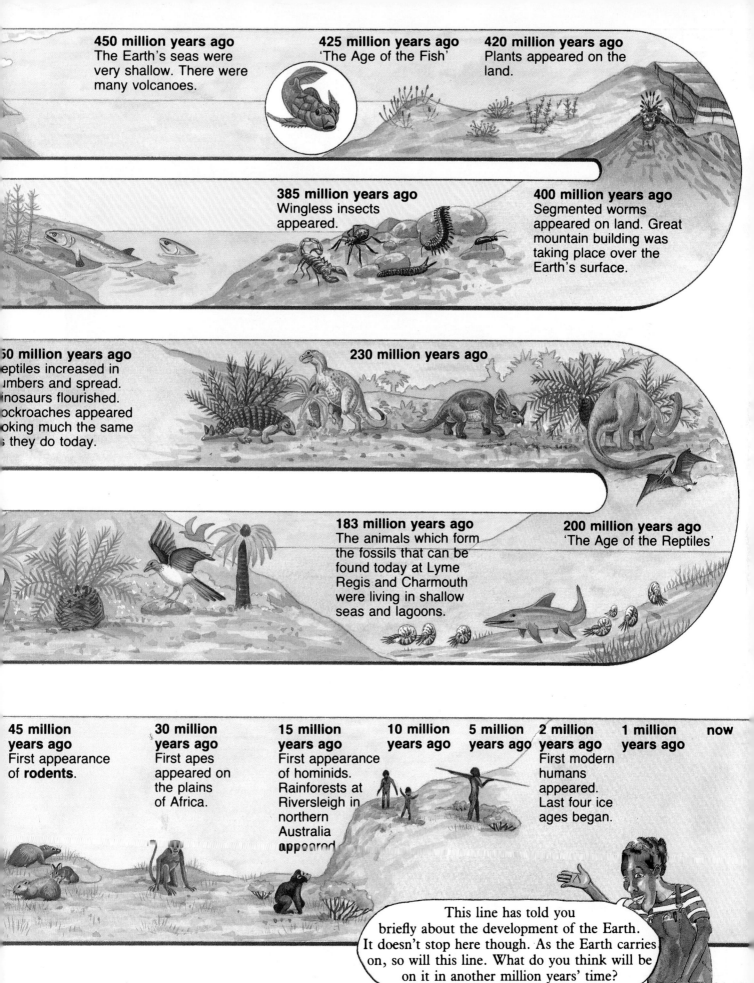

450 million years ago
The Earth's seas were very shallow. There were many volcanoes.

425 million years ago
'The Age of the Fish'

420 million years ago
Plants appeared on the land.

385 million years ago
Wingless insects appeared.

400 million years ago
Segmented worms appeared on land. Great mountain building was taking place over the Earth's surface.

50 million years ago
Reptiles increased in numbers and spread. Dinosaurs flourished. Cockroaches appeared looking much the same as they do today.

230 million years ago

183 million years ago
The animals which form the fossils that can be found today at Lyme Regis and Charmouth were living in shallow seas and lagoons.

200 million years ago
'The Age of the Reptiles'

45 million years ago
First appearance of **rodents**.

30 million years ago
First apes appeared on the plains of Africa.

15 million years ago
First appearance of hominids. Rainforests at Riversleigh in northern Australia appeared.

10 million years ago

5 million years ago

2 million years ago
First modern humans appeared. Last four ice ages began.

1 million years ago

now

This line has told you briefly about the development of the Earth. It doesn't stop here though. As the Earth carries on, so will this line. What do you think will be on it in another million years' time?

11

Fossils

These fossils are of bony fish. Their ancestors had skeletons of soft cartilage, but these fish had hard bones, scaly skins and strong fins.

These are two whelks. The one on the left is a present-day whelk. The one on the right is a fossil and is about one and a half million years old.

This is an ammonite fossil. Ammonites were molluscs which lived in the sea and had coiled shells. The modern day octopus and squid are related to ammonites.

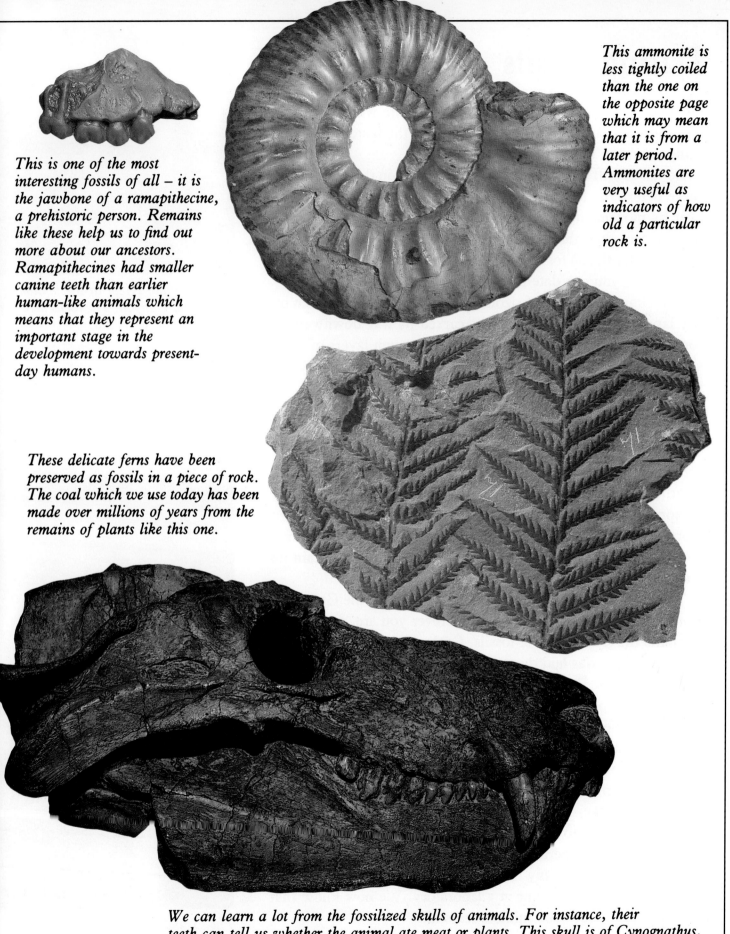

This is one of the most interesting fossils of all – it is the jawbone of a ramapithecine, a prehistoric person. Remains like these help us to find out more about our ancestors. Ramapithecines had smaller canine teeth than earlier human-like animals which means that they represent an important stage in the development towards present-day humans.

This ammonite is less tightly coiled than the one on the opposite page which may mean that it is from a later period. Ammonites are very useful as indicators of how old a particular rock is.

These delicate ferns have been preserved as fossils in a piece of rock. The coal which we use today has been made over millions of years from the remains of plants like this one.

We can learn a lot from the fossilized skulls of animals. For instance, their teeth can tell us whether the animal ate meat or plants. This skull is of Cynognathus, an early mammal resembling a dog which was probably a meat-eater.

13

Dating fossils

How do we know when the plant or creature which is now a fossil was actually living? How can we get the history of living things into the right order?

Look at a cliff or a bank of earth. The layer on the bottom was there before the layer above. Unless the rock has been folded over by movements in the Earth's crust, the layer on the top is more recent than the layers below. So, a fossil in the bottom layer is older than a fossil found above it. If you know the age of rocks, then you can date the fossils in them.

The Grand Canyon in Arizona, USA is the deepest trench on dry land. The Colorado River has carved its way downwards, for one and a half kilometres in places, through layers of sandstone and limestone. The sandstones at the top, where the tourists stand gazing at the view, are 200 million years old. As well as insect and fern fossils, visitors can see the fossilized tracks of reptiles there, preserved in the rock. Halfway down the canyon, in the steep wall of 400 million year-old limestones, are the bones of fish which swam encased in armour plating. Further down, among 500 million year-old rocks, the fish disappear and the only signs of life are traces of shells and worms — animals without backbones. At the bottom, by the river, the rocks are 2000 million years old and they contain no traces of plant or animal life.

There are clear layers of different rocks, as in the Grand Canyon, right across the world. Wherever you are, each layer contains the same kinds of fossils. Geologists decided that each of these layers was laid down at a certain period of time in the Earth's history. Each period of time was given a name. For example, the period of time when dinosaurs lived on the Earth was called the 'Cretaceous period'. The 'Carboniferous period' was the name given to the period when much of the world was warm and covered with swampy forests, some of which turned into the enormous underground stores of coal, oil and natural gas we use today. However, until fairly recently, scientists didn't know how to date rocks so they were unable to tell how long each of these periods of time actually lasted.

Today the age of many rocks, as well as the remains of living things, can be worked out in a laboratory. We now know that the Earth is about 4500 million years old.

The Colorado River at the bottom of the Grand Canyon. The rocks here are 2000 million years old.

The Grand Canyon

Layers of rocks in the Grand Canyon

Plants and animals contain a substance known as carbon-14. By measuring the amount of carbon-14 in an object, it is possible to calculate how much time has passed since the plant or animal from which it was made, died.

Scientists have been able to work out the approximate age of much of the Earth. For example, the oldest rocks so far found on the Earth are in northern Canada. They have been dated as almost 4000 million years old. Some grains of rock have been found in Australia which have been dated at 4300 million years old.

Even with modern technology, however, much of the Earth's history is not known. Geological events are always dated in millions of years which gives plenty of room for error!

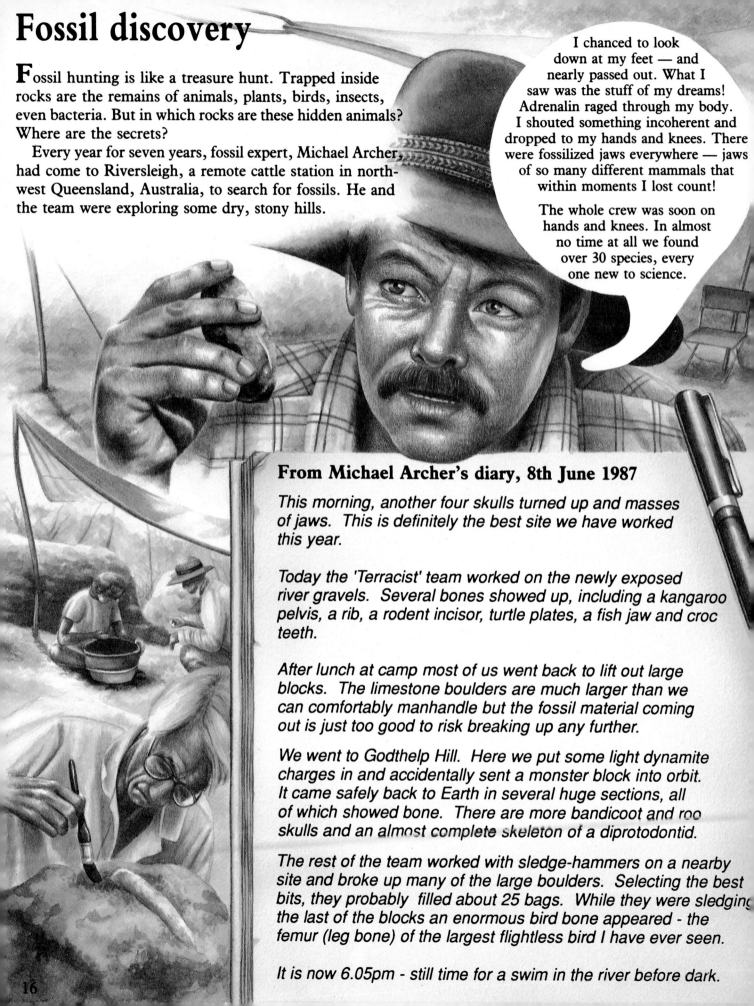

Fossil discovery

Fossil hunting is like a treasure hunt. Trapped inside rocks are the remains of animals, plants, birds, insects, even bacteria. But in which rocks are these hidden animals? Where are the secrets?

Every year for seven years, fossil expert, Michael Archer, had come to Riversleigh, a remote cattle station in north-west Queensland, Australia, to search for fossils. He and the team were exploring some dry, stony hills.

I chanced to look down at my feet — and nearly passed out. What I saw was the stuff of my dreams! Adrenalin raged through my body. I shouted something incoherent and dropped to my hands and knees. There were fossilized jaws everywhere — jaws of so many different mammals that within moments I lost count!

The whole crew was soon on hands and knees. In almost no time at all we found over 30 species, every one new to science.

From Michael Archer's diary, 8th June 1987

This morning, another four skulls turned up and masses of jaws. This is definitely the best site we have worked this year.

Today the 'Terracist' team worked on the newly exposed river gravels. Several bones showed up, including a kangaroo pelvis, a rib, a rodent incisor, turtle plates, a fish jaw and croc teeth.

After lunch at camp most of us went back to lift out large blocks. The limestone boulders are much larger than we can comfortably manhandle but the fossil material coming out is just too good to risk breaking up any further.

We went to Godthelp Hill. Here we put some light dynamite charges in and accidentally sent a monster block into orbit. It came safely back to Earth in several huge sections, all of which showed bone. There are more bandicoot and roo skulls and an almost complete skeleton of a diprotodontid.

The rest of the team worked with sledge-hammers on a nearby site and broke up many of the large boulders. Selecting the best bits, they probably filled about 25 bags. While they were sledging the last of the blocks an enormous bird bone appeared - the femur (leg bone) of the largest flightless bird I have ever seen.

It is now 6.05pm - still time for a swim in the river before dark.

More than 150 new kinds of ancient animals have now been discovered at Riversleigh. The insects, birds, reptiles and fish of 15 million years ago are becoming familiar. But Riversleigh has even more fossil treasures. As one of the experts says, 'It's a layer cake of time.' Where a river used to flow, the remains of animals that lived and died only 50 000 years ago are preserved in soft muds. So scientists can study how the creatures of the area changed through thousands and millions of years.

Volunteers of all ages help at Riversleigh. Enough fossils wait there undiscovered to keep them and the experts busy for a long, long time.

Fifteen million years ago, thick, lush rainforests covered this part of northern Australia. Animals pushed through the mosses and ferns on the shadowy forest floor, searching for food. Some pools and lakes had dangerous edges which gave way when an animal stepped out to drink. Struggling in the water, the drowning animal was torn apart and eaten by lurking crocodiles and turtles. Teeth and bones drifted down to the muddy bottom.

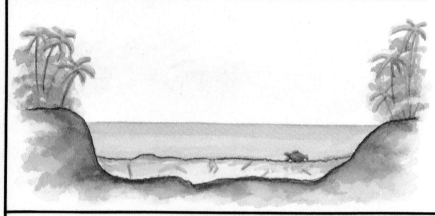

Limestone in the water cemented the bits of animal in the mud. More bones and teeth drifted down — sometimes whole animals or drowned insects, dead birds, old turtles. Very slowly, chemicals in the water altered the chemicals in the once-living matter. Bone and tooth enamel slowly changed into fossil bone and fossil tooth. The shapes stayed exactly the same. Gradually, the layers of limestone thickened. The pools and lakes became shallow.

The climate was changing. The green rainforests died and some of the rainforest animals moved away searching for conditions which suited them. Some altered their habits and bodies as adaptations to the new climate. Some failed to survive and died out. Hot winds swept across dry plains. Summer rains alternated with winter dryness.

Today the 15 million-year-old ponds and lakes of the rainforest are patches of light-grey coloured limestone. They are surrounded by much older dark-grey limestones formed 530 million years ago when the area was covered by a vast, shallow, inland sea.

How are the fossils released from the stone?

The 15 million-year-old ponds do not give up their secrets easily. That light-coloured limestone is incredibly hard. The geologists, zoologists and palaeontologists at Riversleigh have had to develop ways of getting at the fossils. They use explosives to crack the huge boulders and crowbars to prize them apart. Sweating muscle-power heaves the dusty, razor-edged lumps. An ex-army truck donated by the Australian Geographic Society and christened the 'Bonesmobile' and sometimes a rented helicopter help carry the rocks on their long journey from the remote cattle station to distant laboratories.

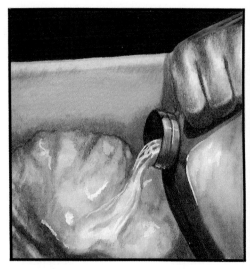

1 *In the laboratory, pieces of limestone are soaked in a weak acid solution.*

2 *Gradually, as the limestone dissolves, delicate fossils begin to appear, sticking up out of their prison in sharp, clear detail.*

Every three days, the limestone is taken out of the acid. Any bones showing are coated with acid-resistant glue to protect them.

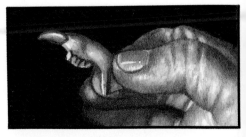

3 *After nine days in the acid bath, a little possum jaw is free from its packaging of hard limestone.*

18

Like careful detectives, scientists can recreate the 15 million-year-old users of the rainforest. Even small fragments of bone, or two or three teeth, can tell much about the animal they once belonged to, what it ate, its size, its habits. The position and shape of jaw muscles can be worked out by muscle scars still visible on the surface of the skull. Scientists compare fossil bones with the bones of living creatures and extinct species, to work out what the creatures at Riversleigh may have looked like 15 million years ago.

Huge seven-metre-long pythons slithered among the creepers and vines. Stabbing-toothed marsupial lions, the size of large dogs, lay along the branches of trees. The rainforest teemed with animals, some extraordinarily different from anything we know. 'Thingodonta', a strange, rabbit-sized creature probably scurried through the leaf litter searching for insects and eggs. Meat-eating kangaroos ripped open possums. Giant flightless birds, ghost bats, frogs, lung-fish, millipedes — the fossil remains have been found, in their thousands.

How rocks are formed

Pick up a rock. Ask yourself where it came from. Every single rock on this Earth has a story, locked up in its shape and appearance. Each has a history of journeys. Some have been squeezed and changed under great pressure or tremendous heat. Some are made from parts of older rocks or once-living creatures. Some have spent millions of years beneath the seas. Some have just appeared for the first time from under the ground. Rocks are the building blocks of our planet. They are not necessarily hard or big. Clay and sand, for example, are both forms of rock.

During the Earth's history, movements in the crust have lifted newly formed layers of rock and folded them as part of high mountains. Then rain, frost and ice, the heat of the sun and the cutting power of the wind began their work of wearing away the exposed rock, breaking it up into boulders, gravel, sand and dust.

This piece of pudding-stone looks as if small pebbles have been stuck in a kind of cement.

Millions of years ago the pebbles were being shovelled by the tides up and down a shingly beach.

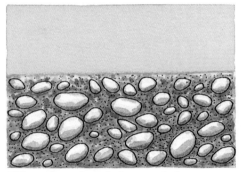

Silt and sand settled around the pebbles.

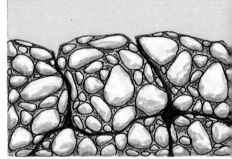

Gradually, the particles bound together forming hard stone. The little pebbles were held like raisins in a pudding.

Each little pebble in a piece of pudding-stone has its own history. Each was once part of a separate rock formed at a particular time and place on the Earth. Each certainly came from hard rock because it survived as a pebble when other softer rocks were destroyed. One pebble might have started in the lava flow of a mighty volcanic explosion. One might have cooled slowly, deep underground. One might even be all that is left of a much earlier piece of pudding-stone.

Rocks are made of minerals. A mineral is a natural, non-living substance with a special chemical make-up. Minerals can be tiny grains or large lumps and they vary in shape. Some rocks are composed of several different types of minerals; others are made from just one type.

Azurite, a copper ore

The minerals in rocks usually form in solid shapes called crystals. Crystals are regular shapes with smooth, flat faces. If a liquid cools slowly, large or coarse crystals form. When a liquid cools fast, the crystals tend to be tiny. If crystals are allowed to form freely, they create exact, geometric shapes but normally the crystals in a rock are fighting for space. Perfect crystals only form in perfect conditions.

As you may remember from the Year 4 Ginn Science book called 'Rocks', there are three main groups of rock:

Quartz crystal

Igneous rocks

Most of the rocks in the Earth's crust are igneous. They are formed from hot molten rock called magma which creeps and seethes deep in the crust or upper mantle. Igneous rocks are the original rocks of the Earth. In some places, where the cover of other rocks has been worn away, we can see old igneous rocks sticking out of the ground. The most common types of rocks formed from magma are granites. These hard rocks are usually speckled with black, cream and white, sometimes with pink and red colours mixed in.

When magma begins cooling under the ground to make granite, the first mineral to crystallize is feldspar. It is a white or creamy-pink colour in its crystallized form. As the magma cools further, colourful crystals of quartz form between the feldspar crystals. Finally, little black specks of mica crystallize, dotting the surface of the rock. If metals are present in the magma, each crystallizes at its own temperature to give the granite a special colour and appearance.

Where magma spurts up out of the ground through the vents of volcanoes, or cracks in the crust, it forms lava. Lava cools into dark-grey or black igneous rock known as basalt. In certain places under the sea, magma seeps out of faults in the crust and creates basalt along the sea-bed.

Magma which flows out on to the ground as lava cools very fast. This makes the crystals in basalt, the rock made from lava, so small that they can only be seen with a microscope. Basalt is sometimes filled with tiny holes made by gas bubbles. If it is really light and frothy, it makes pumice stone. Many people use pumice stone in the bath to remove dead skin from the soles of their feet.

(Below) Cross-section through a volcano

lava

magma

Sedimentary rocks

Rocks like pudding-stone and limestone are called sedimentary rocks. They form on the surface of the Earth, often under water. They are made out of bits of existing rocks, or once-living material, or dissolved minerals. They usually form in layers. Many contain fossils.

Sedimentary rocks are divided up according to the size of the grains that form them. Pudding-stone is made up of large pieces of material. Sandstone is made of middle-sized grains of quartz cemented together with particles of other minerals. Shale is made of layers of clay which have been squeezed together so that all the water has been driven out. The grains in shale are very fine. Chalk is made of countless fragments of tiny shells which are so minute that you need a microscope to see them. Only one-twentieth of all the rocks in the top 16 kilometres of the Earth's crust are sedimentary but they are the ones we see most often because they were formed at the Earth's surface. They make up three-quarters of the world's land area. They provide much evidence of the Earth's nature many millions of years ago. They are also important because they provide oil, natural gas, coal and building stone.

Layers of chalk and flint

Make your own sedimentary rock
- Fill about two-thirds of a clear plastic container with water.
- Mix some sand and dry plaster of Paris or Polyfilla powder in a separate container. You should mix three parts of sand to one part of plaster of Paris or Polyfilla.
- Hold a strong cardboard tube at an angle in the container with one end under the water. Leave a gap between the bottom of the tube and the bottom of the container.
- Slowly pour the mixture down the tube.
- What is happening? Can you see any layers forming?

Metamorphic rocks

Sometimes great heat or pressure changes rocks which have already been formed. These rocks are called 'metamorphic' which means changed shape. Marble is a metamorphic rock formed from limestone which has been exposed to very high temperatures.

1 There are many different types of marble. This piece of marble began 400 million years ago in warm, shallow seas.

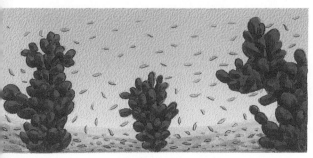

2 Vast numbers of little creatures lived among branching coral reefs. As they died, their bodies drifted down through the water.

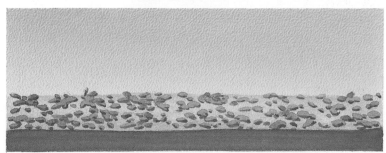

3 The calcium carbonate in their shells and bony parts was deposited in layers on the sea-bed along with bits of dead coral.

4 Gradually, the layers pressed together, building up into thick beds of limestone.

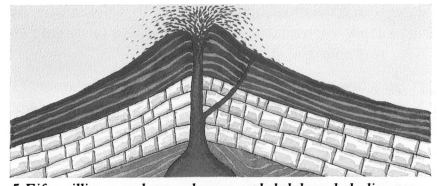

5 Fifty million years later, volcanoes exploded through the limestone. The immense heat changed the limestone, altering the crystals and turning it into marble.

The beautiful swirls of colour, the stains and veins which make the polished surface of a piece of marble so attractive, come from the violent heat and pressure which 'cooked' the remains of sea creatures, coral and traces of minerals in the original limestone rock.

6 Shale can be changed by pressure into the metamorphic rock, slate. During mountain-building, the flaky minerals in shale can be squeezed so hard that they re-crystallize in different directions. This is why slate can be split so easily into thin sheets like the ones used to roof houses.

Crystals

Crystals have always had a magical quality. We find their beautiful shapes in stories and legends. Early man believed that crystals were very hard pieces of ice that would never melt. Fortune-tellers claim to predict our future from their crystal balls. Superman can only be overcome by those who possess the mysterious crystal, Kryptonite. Precious jewels such as diamonds and emeralds are glittering crystals and metals such as gold, silver and platinum all owe their beauty to the pure crystals in them.

Crystals can be perfect in shape, transparent and clear. They are pure in colour and pure in line and form.

Looking at crystals

Many solids — for example, metals, rocks like granite, plaster, diamonds, and even medicine tablets — are made of crystals. The crystals that you might find at school or at home such as salt, bath salts, sugar and sand are fairly transparent. They are also fairly safe and easy to explore.

- Tip a few salt or sugar crystals on to black paper. You could also try crystals of tartaric acid, washing soda and bath salts but remember that these are not for tasting!
- Use a magnifying glass to examine their shapes. How do they differ? How are they the same?
- Draw some of your crystals.

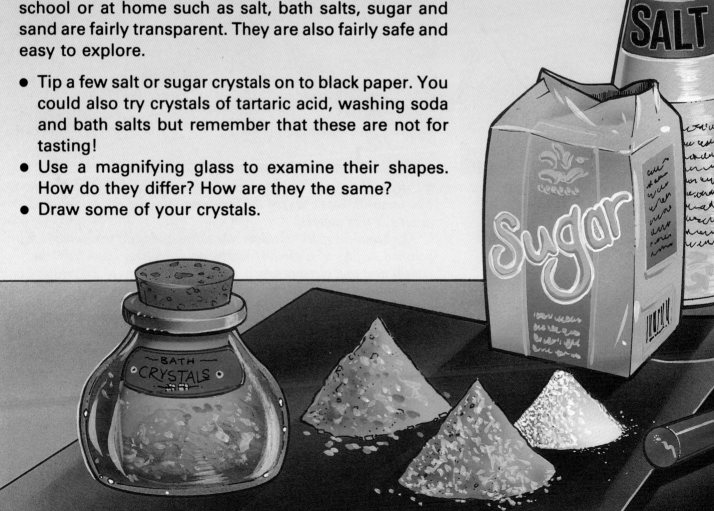

Making crystals

- Try making a solution that is strong enough to form crystals. Add salt to water until it won't dissolve any more. A solution of crystals in water that won't take any more is called a 'saturated solution'.
- Add another spoonful of salt and stir well. Pour a little of the salt solution into a saucer and leave it on a windowsill or another warm place.

You should find that the salt will form crystals again as the water evaporates. If you look at them carefully you will find that they are all the same shape. They are all the same shape as the crystals that you started with too.

You will have many crystals. Each one has formed around a single 'seed' — a tiny crystal too small to see. Each seed has produced one large crystal.

- What would happen if you had only one seed in the crystal solution? Would you end up with one giant crystal? Try it. You might find it works more successfully with alum than with other kitchen crystals like salt.
- What happens if you use a mixture of crystals? For example, what happens if you mix salt and sugar together?

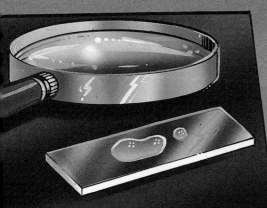

Watching crystals grow

You can actually watch crystals grow.

- Put a drop of your crystal solution on a piece of clear plastic cut from a plastic bottle.
- Put it under a strong lens or a binocular microscope and watch what happens to the drop as the water evaporates.
- Does the crystal grow faster if you warm the plastic on a radiator first? Why?

Rocks in our lives

We don't really notice rocks but they are everywhere in both the natural and built environments. Almost everything in our complex, technological lives depends on rocks.

The soil in which everything grows, including most of the food we eat, is mainly powdered rock. Once humans sheltered in rock caves. They painted scenes on the cave walls with paints made from crushed, coloured rocks. Now we live in artificial caves made of brick, cement, concrete, steel and glass. Bricks are made of clay, a finely powdered rock, baked at high temperature. Cement is limestone mixed with clay heated to a high temperature and ground up into a powder. Concrete is cement with sand and stones added. Steel is made from iron ore. Glass is made from sand melted at high temperature.

Brick houses

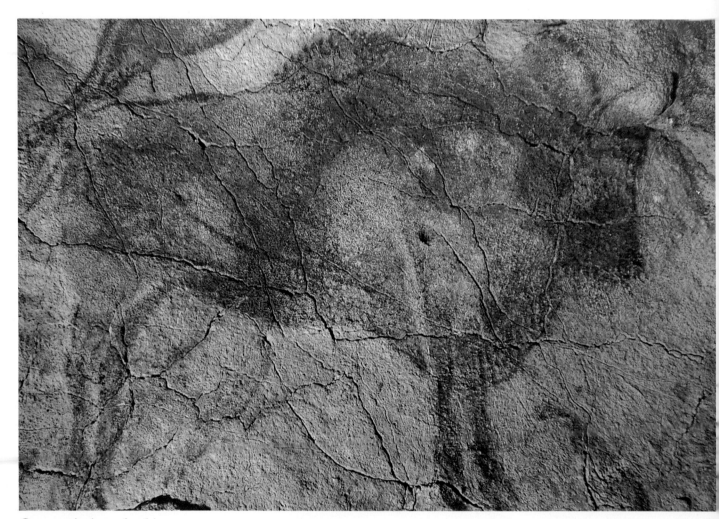

Cave painting of a bison

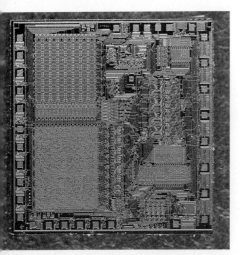

Silicon chip from a computer

Salt pans near the sea in Spain

Gold nugget

Nearly all the metals which we use come from rocks. Coal and oil trapped in sedimentary rocks are fuels as well as the raw materials for the plastics and chemical industries. Even the silicon to make the chips which operate our computers, washing-machines and digital watches comes from sand. The uranium needed for nuclear power is mined as lumps of brownish-black or grey rock. In many parts of the world, salt is made by letting sea water into beach pools at high tide. The sea water is trapped and left to evaporate. Then the salt is collected.

Most rocks in the Earth's crust are of real value to us. Some, though, have been given special value by humans. These rocks are sometimes very rare, sometimes very beautiful and often both. Gemstones such as diamonds, sapphires and rubies; beautiful metals such as gold and silver; and important metals such as iron and copper have all become particularly valuable.

Seams of pure gold occasionally run like veins through white quartz. In some parts of the world the quartz sticks up above the ground and the soft yellow gold can be levered out with a knife. But usually the rock containing the gold has been weathered and broken up. Bits of rock holding their cargo of gold are washed into streams. The rocks continue breaking into smaller pieces. The heavier gold sinks to the bottom of the water. Some pieces are as small as rice grains and some of the gold is as fine as dust.

People pay a high price for gold. Last century, hundreds of thousands of people rushed to California and Australia to look for gold nuggets in river-beds and to scrape gold out of rocks. Nowadays, there is very little gold left on the Earth's surface. Most gold lies deep under the ground and is very difficult to mine.

The metals we use are usually found mixed with other minerals in rocks. They have to be separated out. The first attempts to extract metals from rocks hundreds of years ago were slow and inefficient. Today, modern technology means that enormous amounts of rock can be taken out of the Earth and processed to get the metals and minerals we need. The problem now is that we are fast using up the Earth's supplies of some important minerals. We have used more minerals in the last 50 years than have been used in the whole of human history. We have dramatically changed the surface of the Earth's crust.

Fossil fuels

Find out how your home or school is heated during the winter. What makes the radiators hot or the fires burn? You may find that there is a boiler which runs on either natural gas or oil or there may be a coal fire. All these sources of energy are called fossil fuels. They were formed millions of years ago from the remains of plants and creatures. Some heating systems run on electricity but many of the power stations which produce electricity burn coal.

Oil

Millions of years ago, the only living things on the Earth were millions of tiny, floating, marine plants and creatures called **plankton**. When they died, their bodies settled in huge layers on the sea-bed. Gradually, sedimentary rocks formed around and above the remains of the plankton. The great weight of these rocks put pressure on the dead plankton. This pressure, combined with heat from inside the Earth, slowly changed chemicals, called carbon and **hydrogen**, in the remains into tiny droplets of thick, sludgy liquid which we call crude oil.

There are many oil fields with oil rigs built on them in the North Sea between the United Kingdom and Scandinavia.

Most of the world's oil is still trapped beneath the surface of the Earth in oil fields. Many are beneath the sea. Oil rigs have to be constructed to extract oil. They have huge drills which can go deep into the rock. Drilling rigs are used to try to find new reserves of oil too.

The crude oil that is pumped from a well is very dark and thick. Once oil has been pumped to the surface, it usually has to be refined before it can be made into other products. Different parts of crude oil are used to make different substances. When the oil is refined, these parts are separated from each other. Then it can be made into all sorts of products ranging from petrol to plastic to synthetic fibres.

Natural gas

Natural gas is often found in the same areas as oil. Some of the plankton became gas instead of oil but no one is quite sure why. Natural gas is also found in other sedimentary rocks which contain the remains of plants and creatures which lived on the land.

Oil refinery

Coal

Have you ever put anything on a compost heap? Many gardeners put all their dead plants and grass cuttings on a compost heap. Gradually, as more and more garden waste is added to the top of the heap and as rain falls on it, the material below rots and turns into a dark, wet substance called compost. Gardeners normally dig this back into the soil as it is full of nutrients and acts like a fertilizer.

Coal was formed in a similar way millions of years ago when much of Europe, Asia and North America was covered with thick, swampy forests. As the trees and plants died, their remains rotted and piled up. Before these remains had completely finished rotting, mud and sand covered the material. Slowly, over millions of years, the mud and sand became rock and squeezed all the water out of the decaying debris to leave solid masses of peat. Eventually, the peat hardened into coal.

Coal has been used for centuries. Until recently, it was the most important source of fuel. Nowadays, it is processed to make plastics, fertilizers, paints, road-building materials and even perfume!

Compost heap

All life on the Earth depends on the sun. All the plants and animals whose remains became fossil fuels used the sun's energy to grow. When we use coal, oil or natural gas to produce heat or electricity, we are using some of the energy from the sun that has been trapped for millions of years.

Peat bog in Ireland

The future of fossil fuels

No one knows exactly how much coal, oil or natural gas is left beneath the Earth's surface. Some may still be being formed but there aren't many swampy forests or seas of plankton left now. So scientists are always on the look out for new forms of energy, for example, from the sun, wind and water including waves and tides. The good thing about these resources is that they are renewable — they won't run out. We just have to find ways of using them efficiently. Nuclear power is also used these days but that needs uranium which comes from certain types of rocks which may also be in short supply in the future.

You can read more about fossil fuels and renewable energy in the Ginn Science Year 6 book called 'Water Power and Electricity'.

When coal was first used, most of it was mined from near the surface of the Earth. Nowadays, there is not much coal left near the surface so most is extracted from huge, modern mines deep under the ground.

Space

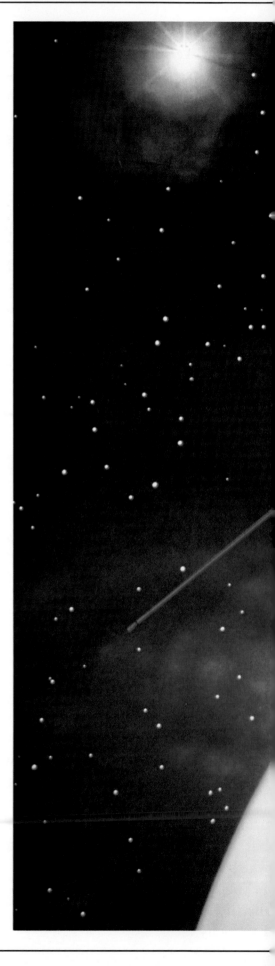

How did the universe begin? What happened before that? Will it end? Does space go on forever? How was our solar system formed? How did life begin on the Earth? Does life exist anywhere else?

Questions like these have puzzled and excited the greatest scientists. We don't know the answers to all these questions but we are finding out a lot more about the universe in which we live. This is a time of important discoveries. New information pours in. Old ideas have to be changed. Astronomers argue and suggest theories. Part of the excitement is the uncertainty. Most of the universe is still waiting to be explored.

We have begun to explore space. The only place humans have visited beyond the Earth is the moon. But our unmanned spacecraft are travelling further and further from our small planet. The instruments they carry are becoming more and more complex and sophisticated. They can map the surface of a distant planet, carry out experiments with the soil and find out which gases are in its atmosphere. Spacecraft can send photographs of its rocks and craters millions of kilometres back to the Earth. For the first time we can see what some of the dots in the sky actually look like from close up.

Fantastic, astonishing discoveries are being made. Each body in our solar system has its own extraordinary character. Each carries the evidence of things which have happened to it and are happening now. Some look bright; some are dim and black. Most large objects in the solar system are round but some of the smaller moons around planets are oddly shaped, often looking like lumpy potatoes. Some worlds have no atmosphere around them; others have atmospheres with violent winds and even thunder and lightning like on the Earth. Some have rocky surfaces; some shine with thick ice. Some have massive mountains which dwarf anything here on the Earth. Some have a cloak of gases wrapped around them. Some tumble slowly; others spin very fast.

Everything we learn about the other bodies orbiting the sun helps us understand our planet better. Our space probes have now flown past or landed on every known planet in the solar system except Pluto. New and wonderful moons have been discovered. Much more waits to be explored.

The sun and the solar system

What is our own tiny piece of the universe like? What do we know about our little bit of space?

The nearest star to us here on the Earth is so close that we can damage our eyes if we look at it directly. Explosions of hot gas flare hundreds of thousands of kilometres out from its glaring yellow surface. Every second inside the furnace of its huge core, about four million tonnes of hydrogen gas are turned into helium. The heat and light given off makes the star shine. The energy flows out in every direction. Some of this energy goes past our planet and heats it and floods it with light. Without this star, nothing could live on the Earth.

This star is over a million times bigger than the Earth. Yet, it is actually quite an ordinary, average-sized star, about halfway through its life with enough fuel for another 5000 million years or so.

The star you have been reading about is, of course, the sun. Travelling around the sun are the planets, often with moons orbiting around them. All these objects are lit by the sun and do not give out any of their own visible light and heat. All the planets, large and small, near and far from the sun, are held from drifting away into space by the pull of the sun's gravity. The sun, planets and moons make up our solar system.

The famous English scientist, Sir Isaac Newton, said that the force of gravity causes every object in the universe to attract or be attracted to every other object. The force of gravity is stronger the more massive the objects and it is stronger the closer the objects are to each other. But we can only feel ourselves being pulled by gravity towards another object when that object is really huge, like a planet or a moon. Ordinary, everyday things, like the objects around us, are far too small for us to notice any pull towards them.

The Earth's force of gravity causes objects to fall to the ground. It also causes the moon and satellites to orbit the Earth, just as the sun's gravity causes the Earth and the other planets to orbit it. The moon circles the Earth once every 29.5 days and is a fiftieth of its volume.

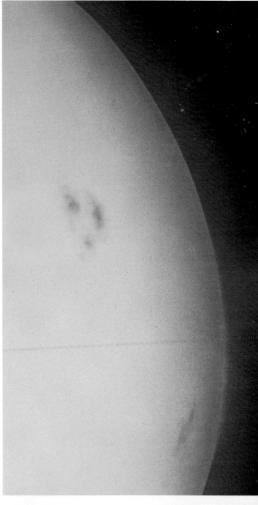

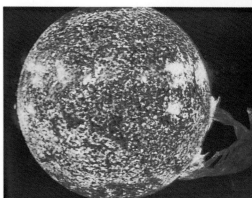

These pictures show flares of hot gas coming off the surface of the sun.

Under no circumstances must we ever look at the sun through a magnifying glass, telescope or binoculars as this would blind us instantly.

If we could look down on our solar system from above our North Pole, we would see the planets orbiting the sun in nearly circular paths, in an anti-clockwise direction. As far as we know, every planet except Venus spins on its axis this way round too. Most of the moons orbit and spin in the same anti-clockwise direction.

Our solar system is only a minute piece of the universe. Our sun is only one star among countless millions of stars. Yet, even within this minute part of the universe, the distances are enormous. The sun is about 150 million kilometres from the Earth. If we travelled at a steady 100 kilometres an hour, about the speed of a car on a motorway, we would take about 170 years to reach the sun. Even Venus, the nearest planet to the Earth, is 39 million kilometres away from us at its closest. Compared with the vast distances between them, the planets themselves are very small.

The planets are some of the largest objects in the solar system. Most of the planets have objects known as moons or satellites travelling around them.

There are two main groups of planets within our solar system. Four are small and rocky and are much closer to the sun than the other group. Four are huge gas giants moving through the vast emptiness and extreme cold far from the sun. Tiny Pluto, which does not belong to either group, usually orbits furthest away of all.

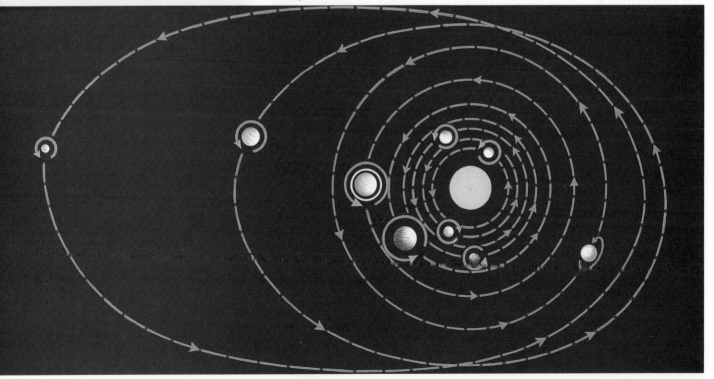

Space exploration

Lift off!

Before humans could explore space, we had to get off the Earth. The pull of the Earth's gravity holds everything — water, atmosphere, soil, rocks, living things — from floating off into space. Blast a firework rocket into the sky and after all the gunpowder fuel has been used up, gravity pulls the stick back down. A rocket with much more fuel will travel much faster and higher. And, if you could make a rocket with enough fuel, the Earth's gravity would not be strong enough to pull it back. The rocket would keep on travelling further and further away from the Earth without stopping.

Satellites

A satellite is an object, either natural or artificial, which orbits around a larger object in space. The Russians sent the first human-made object into orbit around the Earth on 4th October 1957. The satellite, Sputnik 1, was launched by a two-stage rocket. Only a few years before, most people had thought that space exploration was not possible but, after Sputnik 1, they had to change their minds. Since Sputnik, one new satellite has been launched, on average, every three days. You can sometimes see satellites moving steadily across the sky on dark, clear evenings.

To stay up in space for a long time, satellites must orbit high above the atmosphere. If they go below about 500 kilometres, satellites begin to slow down as they hit the top of the atmosphere. Eventually they fall out of orbit and burn up in the upper atmosphere, like meteors. Most satellites orbit higher, between 500 and 2000 kilometres from the Earth's surface. The height at which satellites orbit depends on the job they have to do.

Communications satellites orbit about 35 000 kilometres above the ground over the equator. They transmit television signals, telephone conversations, computer data and pictures of the Earth below. At this height, each satellite orbits the Earth once a day — the same time it takes the Earth to turn beneath it. In this way, the satellite keeps pace with the turning Earth and stays above the same place all the time.

There are about 200 working satellites in space at the moment. They are mostly solar-powered with solar panels that change the sun's light into electricity.

Launch of a satellite

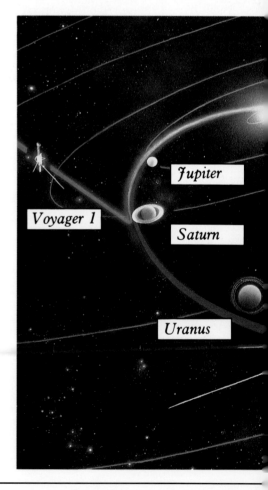

(Below)
Diagram of the paths taken by the Voyager spacecraft

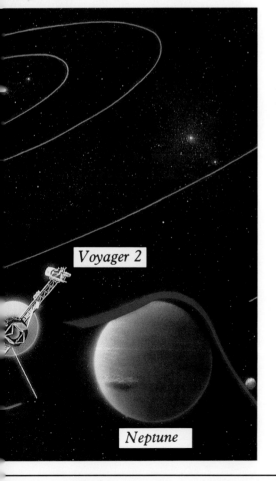

Voyager 2

Neptune

Like most machines, satellites don't last forever. A satellite or any space vehicle which stops working keeps orbiting. If it explodes, all the bits keep on orbiting. We humans have already made space a rubbish dump. Travelling in a band around the Earth are tens of thousands of useless pieces of space junk — bolts, solid fuel boosters, solar cells, cameras, fragments of aluminium and flecks of paint. Space collisions are a real danger. Even a tiny particle of paint can badly damage a spaceship if they collide at tremendous speed.

Space probes

A space probe is an unmanned spacecraft which can send information back to the Earth as it travels in space. In 1977, the Americans launched two space probes, Voyager 1 and Voyager 2, into the solar system and deep space. Since then, both Voyagers have photographed planets and their moons, collected scientific and engineering data and sent information back to the Earth. Voyager 1 reached the area of Jupiter and its moons 18 months after being launched. Twenty months later it made a 'flyby' of Saturn and provided information about its rings and moons. From then on, Voyager 2 took over though Voyager 1 does still send back data. Voyager 2 left Saturn in September 1981 and arrived at Uranus four and a half years later. Three and a half years later, in August 1989, it passed within 5000 kilometres of the furthest of the gas giants, Neptune.

The cameras and instruments of the two Voyagers have extended our knowledge to the distant parts of the solar system. They have discovered much that has always been secret. If all goes well, the Voyagers will stay in contact with the Earth until 2020 when their power supply will run out. But after that, they may continue to travel forever, far away from our solar system, further and further into space. Voyager 2 is due to pass the star Sirius in about 300 000 years' time and Voyager 1 is heading for an encounter with an ageing dwarf star in 40 000 years' time!

In case the Voyagers are ever discovered by aliens, they carry messages from the Earth. They have discs mounted on the outside with natural Earth sounds, music, pictures and greetings in 60 languages recorded in 1977. Scientists hope that aliens would be able to work out how to listen to the message from the President of the United States — 'This is a present from a small distant world.' The messages are designed to last for 100 million years.

The four inner planets

Mercury

Mercury is a scorched, battered little planet, turning on its axis very slowly but taking only 88 days to orbit the sun. If you could stand on Mercury, you would see the sun as a glaring ball appearing almost three times as wide as it does from the Earth. Mercury is made of rock with a metal core. Its surface is pockmarked by craters and covered with dust. There are no volcanoes here, no molten lava flows and there is hardly any atmosphere.

Venus

From the Earth, Venus is the brightest planet in the night sky. A thick blanket of creamy-yellow clouds completely hides its surface. Venus is our nearest neighbour in the solar system and is almost the same size as the Earth. People used to think that there might be life on Venus. Perhaps rain poured down from the clouds. Perhaps dinosaurs roamed in steamy swamps. No one knew what actually happened below the clouds until the Russians managed to parachute scientific instruments down on to Venus' surface in 1975.

They discovered that Venus is very different from the Earth. The clouds rain **sulphuric acid**. There is no water at all. Lightning flashes and thunder rolls and crashes without ceasing. The atmosphere is made of the heavy gas, carbon dioxide, and weighs down with enormous pressure. The carbon dioxide atmosphere prevents the sun's heat escaping from the rocky surface of the planet, rather like the way a greenhouse on Earth keeps in the sun's heat. This 'greenhouse effect' causes the extremely high temperatures on Venus. Venus' surface is hot enough to melt metals.

Venus has rocks similar to the igneous rocks found on the Earth. They crumble in the searing heat. Lava is forced out through vents in the crust. Rugged mountains and rubble-strewn plains shimmer in the heat haze. Although Venus looks a beautiful planet from the outside, we now know that it is very unsuitable for life.

Earth

The Earth is unique within the solar system; it has water as a liquid and an atmosphere that allows life as we know it. The Earth has one natural satellite, the moon.

Surface of Mercury, photographed in 1974 by Mariner 10, an American space probe

Venus

Surface of Venus, photographed in 1982 by Venera 13, a Soviet space probe. Part of the space probe can be seen at the bottom of the photograph.

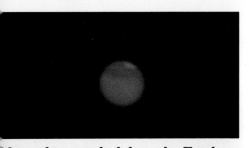
Mars photographed from the Earth through a telescope

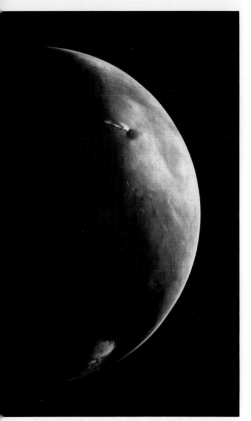
Mars photographed from an American space probe

Mars

Mars is only half the diameter of the Earth and is further from the sun. A day on Mars lasts as long as an Earth day but Mars takes 687 Earth days compared with our 365 to travel around the sun. In other words, a year on Mars is 687 days long. The surface of Mars can usually be observed from the Earth because there are no clouds in its thin atmosphere, only occasional dust storms that can hide the surface for weeks at a time. A hundred years ago, some astronomers thought they saw thin, dark lines on the planet. They wondered if they could be canals made by intelligent beings. Since then, astronomers have realized that these lines are simply optical illusions.

More recently, scientists hoped that there was water on Mars and that it had a usable atmosphere but when American space probes parachuted on to Mars in 1976, they recorded a cold, dust-ridden, desolate place. Endless winds churn the orange-red dust across the rocky plains, turning the sky a salmon-pink colour. Mars has massive, extinct volcanoes and a canyon twice as deep and nine times as long as the Earth's Grand Canyon. As on Venus, the air is made of carbon dioxide but it is very thin and dry. It gives little protection from the sun's deadly ultraviolet rays which bombard the planet. The tests carried out in 1976 did not reveal any life on Mars, not even microscopic life in the red soil.

Space probes have now photographed the whole of Mars' surface. There are no canals but there is water hidden on Mars. Water is trapped as ice, deep under the ground. It is also frozen in the polar ice-caps and is held as part of the minerals in the soil. Mars has seasons like the Earth and the Martian ice-caps get larger and smaller with the Martian winters and summers.

Mars has two little lumpy moons shaped like potatoes. Their surface are black rock, bashed and pock-marked.

Viking 2, an American space probe on the surface of Mars in 1976

Rocky Martian landscape

The four gas giants and Pluto

Jupiter

Mighty Jupiter is the sun's biggest companion in the solar system. It takes eleven and three-quarter Earth years for Jupiter to revolve around the sun. The planet has an atmosphere of nearly liquid hydrogen which presses down on a core of thick, oily, liquid hydrogen. It is difficult to tell where the surface begins and ends. Dense clouds hide Jupiter, swirling in vividly-coloured bands. Little or no sunlight gets through the deep layers of cloud to the surface beneath. Huge storms, with blasts of lightning, shake this extraordinarily alien environment.

Sixteen moons have been discovered around Jupiter. The two biggest are about the size of the planet Mercury. The Voyager space probes sent us the first ever close-up photographs of the four largest moons in 1979. Astronomers were amazed. One moon, Europa, has a strange, smooth surface of water frozen into thick ice, veined with cracks. Io, Jupiter's closest moon, is a ball of yellow and orange-brown rock. The photographs showed live, erupting volcanoes on Jupiter.

Saturn

Saturn is a smaller, colder, calmer version of Jupiter. It is also largely made up of hydrogen which is the lightest element. It is so light that Saturn would float if you could find enough water to put it in! But Saturn is a huge planet, nine and a half times the width of the Earth. Saturn spins so fast it bulges at the middle and night lasts only five hours. Saturn takes almost 30 Earth years to travel around the distant sun. Winter on Saturn is 15 Earth years long. Astronomers think that Saturn, like Jupiter, has a small rocky core at the centre, surrounded by liquid hydrogen. Dense, yellowish clouds stretch across its surface.

Through a telescope from the Earth, Saturn appears to have rings or a halo around it. Close up, they turn out to be thousands of separate rings each filled with pieces of ice or ice-covered material ranging from tiny specks to mini-icebergs tens of metres wide. The rings form a flat disc which is less than two kilometres thick but a quarter of a million kilometres across.

So far, 23 moons have been discovered orbiting around Saturn. They are all very cold and are thought to be rocky often with a covering of ice on their surfaces.

Jupiter and Io, one of its moons

Saturn photographed by Voyager 1

Close-up of Saturn's rings

Uranus

Uranus

Scientists now know that Uranus is a quiet, placid planet four times the width of the Earth. From its cold surface, the sun would appear as a distant, brilliant star 19 times smaller than the sun we see.

Uranus is a pale greenish-blue colour and is tipped on its side. The atmosphere of hydrogen mixed with some helium is heavy and deep. Voyager 2 discovered ten small moons to add to the five strange, large moons astronomers already knew existed.

Neptune

Until Voyager 2 visited Neptune in August 1989, we knew very little about this planet, the furthest of the four 'gas giants' from the sun. We knew Neptune was cold and a little smaller than Uranus with a 165-year-long orbit around the sun. Only two moons had ever been seen even through the strongest telescopes. Now we know that underneath its thick clouds of hydrogen, helium and methane gases, Neptune, like Uranus, is a giant ball of water, ice and liquid methane (natural gas) with a rocky centre. But unlike Uranus, Neptune has incredible, active weather. Winds race around the planet. Giant storms rage in the atmosphere. Clouds of methane float 50 to 100 kilometres above the lower clouds.

Neptune is a beautiful deep blue. Voyager 2 confirmed astronomers' suspicions that there are thin rings round the planet and six more small, very dark moons.

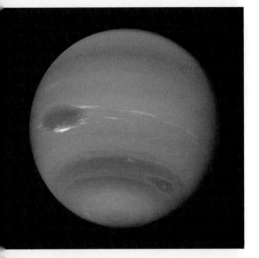

Neptune photographed by Voyager 2

Pluto

In 1930, scientists found the planet, Pluto, out in the distant parts of the solar system. Pluto is smaller than our moon. In 1978, scientists discovered that Pluto has one grey moon, half its own size, which circles it closely.

Pluto takes 248 years to orbit the distant sun. It has a stretched orbit, tilted at a different angle from the other planets. This actually takes it nearer the sun than Neptune for 20 years of its orbit. In fact, until 1999, Neptune is the furthest known planet from the sun. Pluto is made, scientists think, of hard, frozen ices and has a thin atmosphere of methane gas.

There are no photographs of Pluto because no space probes have been close to it. This picture shows what scientists think Pluto and its moon might look like.

Other things in the solar system

Egg-shaped rocks, balls of ice, pellets of iron, bits of dust and debris — objects of all shapes and sizes — move around the solar system. Some are smooth, some are battered and some look as if they have suffered severely in massive collisions.

Asteroids

One large group of rocky objects orbit in a band between the inner and outer planets, between Mars and Jupiter. They are asteroids but they could be thought of as small planets. They vary in size from very small objects to objects 1000 kilometres across. Some are long, some are lumpy, some are much brighter than others. Some tumble over and over. All are made of stone or metals and all are without atmospheres. One, called Pallas, even has a tiny moonlet orbiting around its cratered surface. The band in which most of the asteroids travel is known as the asteroid belt.

Scientists used to think the asteroid belt was crowded with asteroids. But, in fact, if you chose an asteroid to land on in a space ship (and tethered it carefully to stop it floating off again), you would only see your neighbouring asteroid as a distant disc of light.

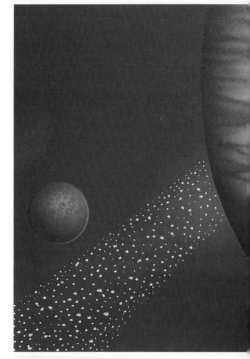

Diagram showing the asteroid belt between Mars and Jupiter

Comets

Comets belong to the distant, frozen parts of the solar system. Made of ice and rocks, they are small, less than 50 kilometres across. Most travel in enormous orbits far beyond the furthest planet. Some occasionally journey in among the inner planets. Here the heat of the sun begins melting the ice. It usually streams out in a huge, brilliantly lit tail of dust and gas millions of kilometres long. Long ago, people used to think that the sight of a comet in the sky was a warning of a disaster coming. Halley's Comet is the most famous comet of all. There are records of sightings of the comet going back over 2000 years. It visits the inner solar system once every 75 years or so. Although hundreds of comets have been seen in the sky throughout history, we now know that these are just a few of the millions that must exist beyond the orbit of Pluto.

Halley's comet as it was last seen in 1986

his tapestry records an appearance of Halley's comet when Harold was crowned King of England in 1066. The met is in the top right corner.

Meteors and meteorites

Meteors are tiny bits of stone or metal, fragments of asteroids, perhaps broken-up comets. During the first 500 million years of the solar system's history, an enormous number of meteors were whizzing around, colliding with planets, moons and asteroids, cratering their surfaces. Today there are fewer meteors and most are smaller than grains of rice. In fact, most are the size of dust particles.

Meteors approaching the Earth burn up in its atmosphere as they plummet towards its surface. As they burn up, they leave a bright flash or streak of light in the night sky. We call them 'shooting stars'. Just occasionally, meteors are large enough to get through the Earth's atmosphere and crash on its surface. Meteors that reach the surface of the Earth are known as meteorites.

Our solar system ends far beyond Pluto and the comets. It ends where the gravity of other stars is stronger than the gravity of the sun and begins to pull objects towards them and away from the sun.

Meteor seen in daylight burning up in the Earth's atmosphere

Amazing measurements

Distances in space are so huge that scientists describe them with special units of measurement.

We use the distance between the sun and the Earth as a way of measuring distance in the solar system. The 150 million kilometres between the sun and the Earth is called one astronomical unit. The Earth is therefore one AU (astronomical unit) from the sun. The next nearest star to the Earth, after the sun, is 270 000 AU away.

Draw or model your own representation of the solar system. Don't try to represent both the planet sizes and their distances from one another on the same scale. Choose one scale for the sizes of the planets and another for their distances from the sun.

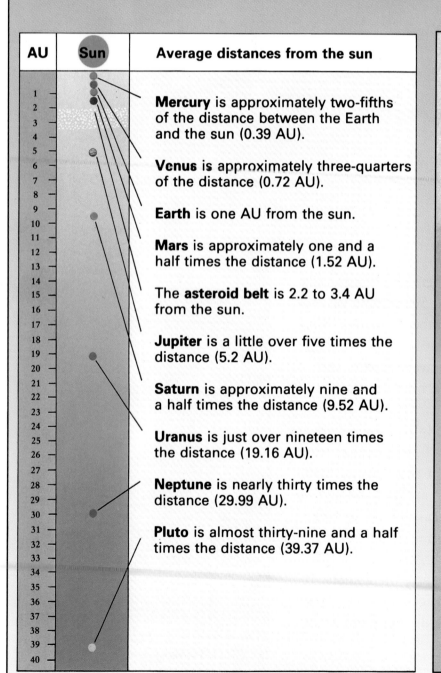

AU	Sun	Average distances from the sun
		Mercury is approximately two-fifths of the distance between the Earth and the sun (0.39 AU).
		Venus is approximately three-quarters of the distance (0.72 AU).
		Earth is one AU from the sun.
		Mars is approximately one and a half times the distance (1.52 AU).
		The **asteroid belt** is 2.2 to 3.4 AU from the sun.
		Jupiter is a little over five times the distance (5.2 AU).
		Saturn is approximately nine and a half times the distance (9.52 AU).
		Uranus is just over nineteen times the distance (19.16 AU).
		Neptune is nearly thirty times the distance (29.99 AU).
		Pluto is almost thirty-nine and a half times the distance (39.37 AU).

Retired

He was tired after his voyages,
the shuttles from planet to planet
from star to star.

In the late evening
he would sway in his rocking chair
and watch the moon through the trees.

'I was there once,' he thought
'I stood on that globe.
Now it is like a football
shining in space.'

And he could hardly believe it
that in his helmet
and in his bulky space suit
he'd stirred that far dust.

Iain Crichton Smith

Planet sizes

The **sun** is 1 400 000 km in diameter, 110 times wider than the Earth.

Jupiter is eleven times larger than the Earth, 143 000 km across.

Saturn is nine and a half times the diameter of the Earth, 120 000 km across.

Uranus is four times bigger than the Earth, with a diameter around 51 800 km.

Neptune is a little less than four times the size of the Earth, around 49 500 km across.

The **Earth** has a diameter of 12 756 km.

Venus is almost the same size as the Earth, 12 100 km across.

Mars is about half the diameter of the Earth, 6794 km across.

Mercury is a bit less than one third the size of the Earth with a diameter of 4880 km.

Pluto is smaller than the moon, 2300 km across.

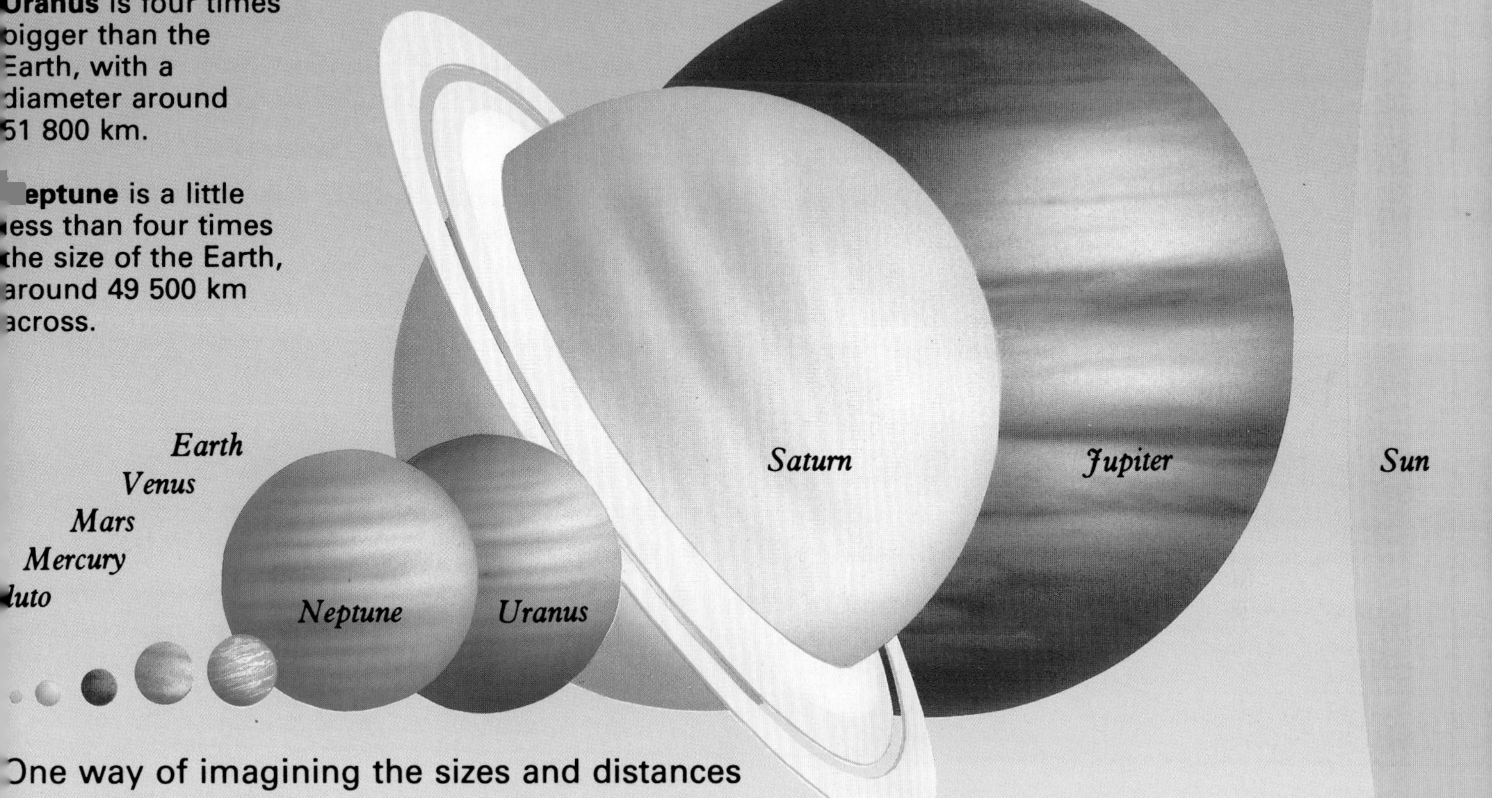

Earth
Venus
Mars
Mercury
Pluto

Neptune   Uranus   Saturn   Jupiter   Sun

One way of imagining the sizes and distances of the solar system is to think of the sun as a beachball with a 60 cm diameter. Then,

Mercury would be a mustard seed 25 m away;
Venus — a pea 47 m away;
Earth — a pea 66 m away;
Mars — a pin's head 102 m away;
Jupiter — an orange 300 m away;
Saturn — a tangerine 600 m away;
Uranus — a plum 1200 m away;
Neptune — an apricot 1800 m away;
Pluto — a sugar granule 2300 m away.

The nearest star to the sun would be another beachball 12 000 km away!

Beyond the solar system

Our sun, with its solar system, is part of a vast collection of stars, dust and gas called a galaxy. When we look at the night sky, practically everything we see belongs to this galaxy which is known as the Milky Way. There are about 100 000 million stars in the Milky Way, but we can only see several thousand of them with our eyes alone, even on the darkest night.

(Below) The Milky Way

Spiral-shaped Andromeda Galaxy

Our galaxy is shaped like a Catherine wheel and is slowly rotating. The sun, the Earth and the rest of the solar system lie about two-thirds out from the galaxy's centre. The centre is hidden by a great dark cloud of dust and gas 250 000 million million (250 000 000 000 000 000) kilometres away.

If we could look through a powerful telescope, we would begin to see more stars — stars behind and beyond the stars of the Milky Way. They belong to other galaxies, each containing another 100 000 million or so stars. Nobody understood that there was more than one galaxy until this century. Now astronomers tell us that there are about 100 thousand million galaxies in the universe. We still do not really know how huge the universe actually is.

To us, stars look like little pin-points of light. But close up, every star in the sky is a great globe of gas glaring with the fierce energy of **nuclear fusion**. Stars can be old, young or just forming. Some are truly huge, some immensely far away. Each star shines with the light of its burning. Light always travels at the same speed, 300 000 kilometres a second. Even then, we can only see the stars as they used to be. The light from the nearest star to us has taken four years to reach us. The light from many stars in the Milky Way travels for thousands of years before it reaches us.

The galaxies are not crowded together. There are vast empty spaces between them and the distances grow all the time because the universe is expanding.

It is almost impossible for us to imagine how many stars there are in the universe or how big the universe is. We do know that there are more stars in the universe than the number of grains of sand on an enormous sandy beach.

Even in our galaxy, millions of stars are probably the same size, age and temperature as our sun. Do any have a solar system like our sun, with planets orbiting around? The problem is that planets are so small, compared with the size and brilliance of a star, that astronomers have not yet managed to see any, except the ones belonging to our own solar system. Yet scientists reckon that planets must exist, perhaps millions of them.

Nobody knows if there is any life anywhere else in the universe. As well as putting messages on the two Voyagers, scientists have sent special radio waves deep into space but they could take thousands of years to make contact with any other life, if it exists.

Constellations

Some stars seem to make patterns in the night sky. For centuries, people all over the world have given the patterns the names of animals, birds, gods, men and women. Many stories have been told about them.

We call these patterns or groups of stars 'constellations'. A very good imagination is needed to see the pictures in the patterns. Shown here, for example, are Leo the Lion and Scorpio the Scorpion.

But the patterns make the complicated sky more familiar and help us find certain stars. Europeans use many of the patterns and names worked out by the Ancient Greeks.

The Earth is like a roundabout and we are like passengers, carried around with it. As the Earth turns, we look out into a different part of space. So, every hour of the night, we see new stars and star patterns coming into view.

The part of the sky we can see at a particular time on a particular night, depends on which day of the year it is and where exactly we are standing on the Earth. We will see one part of the sky if we live in the northern hemisphere and a different part if we live in the southern hemisphere.

Scholars in many countries collected information about the stars. They realized that stars and constellations could be seen in the same part of the sky at the same time each year. The calendar that we use today is based on these ancient studies of star movements.

Measurements

Light travels at 300 000 km per second. Nothing travels faster than light.

Light from the sun reaches the Earth in just over eight minutes. Light crosses our solar system in 11.5 hours, just under half a day. The distance a ray of light travels in one year is called a light-year (LY) and astronomers measure distances in space in light-years. One light-year equals nearly ten million million kilometres (9 460 000 000 000 km).

The nearest star in our galaxy, after the sun, is called Alpha Centauri. It is actually a cluster of three stars and it is 4.3 light-years away (40 million million km). Our galaxy, the Milky Way, is almost 100 000 light-years from one side to the other. Our sun is about 34 000 light-years from the centre of the galaxy.

Slowly, sailors learned to use the 'map of the sky' — where the constellations and stars, the planets and the moon could be seen each night — to help work out where they were in the lonely ocean. Aircraft, until very recently, carried a navigator who calculated the aircraft's position by observing the stars.

We can find where north is, if we live in the northern hemisphere, by learning to recognize some constellations. One bright group of stars, called the Great Bear or the Big Dipper, can always be seen from Europe and North America. Part of the Great Bear constellation is known as the Plough. It is shaped like an old-fashioned wooden plough or saucepan. The stars in the Great Bear constellation are not close to each other. They just look close together to us here on the Earth.

Imagine a line drawn from the end two stars. The line points to a not very bright, unimportant looking star called Polaris, or the pole-star. The pole-star is always due north, wherever we are.

On the other side of the pole-star from the Plough are five stars in a wide 'W' shape. This is the constellation of Casseopeia.

Part of the constellation of Orion can be seen from all parts of the Earth. Betelgeuse, in Orion's armpit, is an enormous red star 3000 times more powerful than our sun. Its surface is relatively cool but would extend out to the orbit of Mars if placed in the position of our sun.

The brightest star in the sky is our sun. It is so bright its light blocks out the light from all other stars. The light from the sun takes eight minutes 20 seconds to reach us. At night, when the sun is not in our half of the sky, the brightest star we can see is Sirius. Sirius is not far from Orion. It is a bit bigger and hotter than our sun. Light from Sirius takes eight and three-quarter years to reach us so we see Sirius as it was nearly nine years ago. The light, after all, has had to travel 8 100 000 000 000 kilometres!

But that isn't much compared with a star like Polaris. The light from the pole-star takes 700 years to reach the Earth. That means the light we see now when we find Polaris in the northern sky left Polaris in medieval days. Go and have a look!

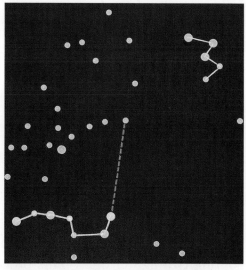

Diagram showing how to find the pole-star from the Great Bear

Constellation of Orion and (below) the figure of Orion marked out by the stars

Glossary

glaciers
A glacier is a very slow-moving river of ice.

hydrogen
The hydrogen that is found on the Earth is a very light and inflammable gas.

nuclear fusion
Nuclear fusion is the creation of a new nucleus by joining two lighter ones. This process releases a huge amount of energy.

plankton
Plankton are very small plants and animals which drift near the surface of seas or lakes.

rodents
Rodents are a large family of mammals with gnawing teeth. This family includes mice, rats, beavers and squirrels.

sponges
A sponge is a water animal with a tough but squashy skeleton. Sponges often live in colonies forming a big spongy mass.

sulphuric acid
Sulphuric acid is a burning, corrosive liquid.